Nature's Small World
By Rick McKeon
Copyright 2015 Rick McKeon

Preface

Looking at nature close up is amazing! It opens up whole new vistas, and you see things you have never seen before. Ordinary objects become extraordinary!

After purchasing a microscope to view stamps and coins on my computer I thought I'd have a look at a leaf. Wow! I was amazed at all of the beauty and detail I had been missing! So, this is my way of sharing some of the wonder and beauty I have found.

This is a collection of beautiful images taken through the microscope and then the same objects at normal size so you can tell what they are. The first half of the book has the close up images and the second half, starting on page 32, has the full size pictures. See if you can guess what they are before looking at the answer. I bet you will be surprised at some of them!

I'd like to give a special thanks to my good friend and fellow writer Dennis Montgomery for his encouragement and suggestions.

This is going to be a journey of discovery, so let's have some fun discovering *Nature's Small World*.

Out in the Field Collecting Samples

Often My Desk Is Covered with Samples to Photograph

Photo 1

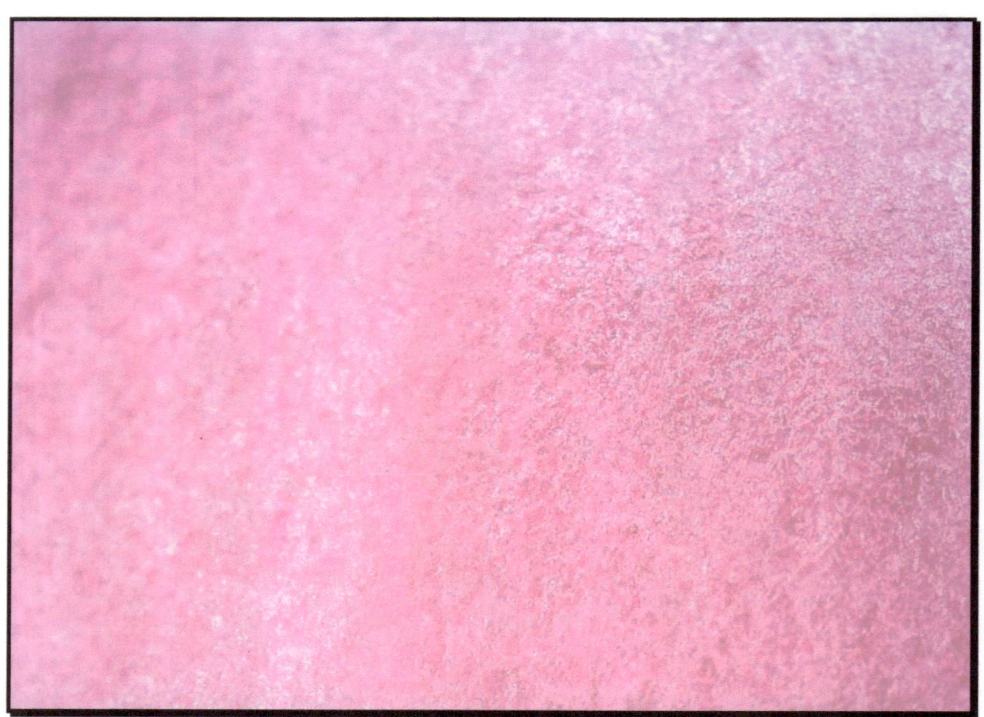

Photo 2

Photo 3

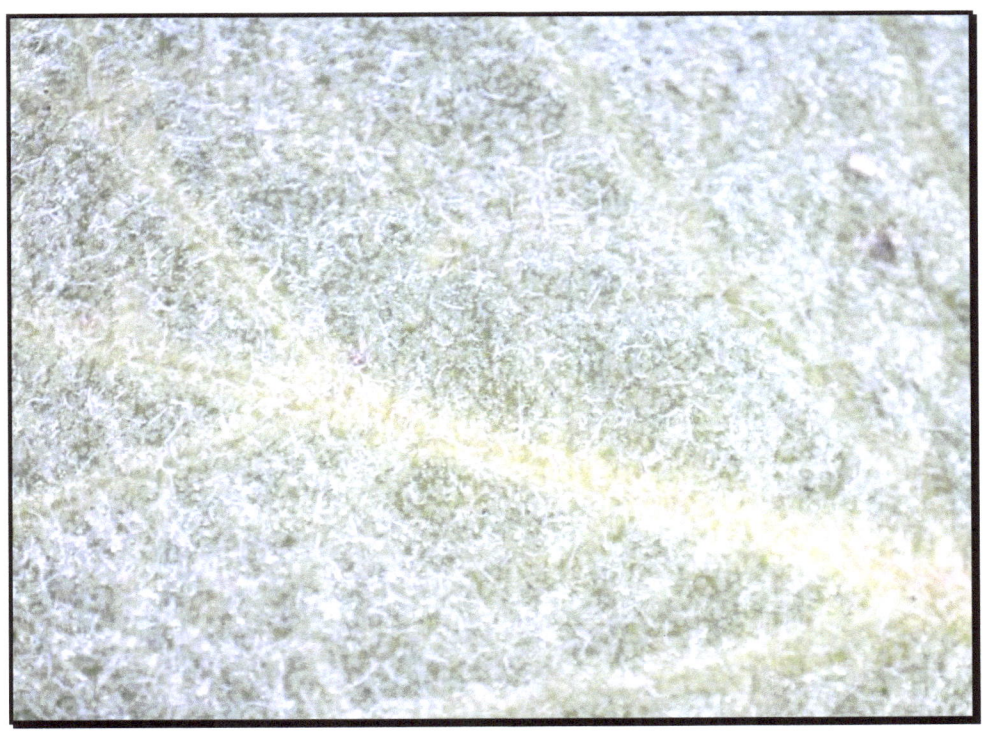

Photo 4

Photo 5

Photo 6

Photo 6 - Same Object with Darker Lighting

Photo 7

Photo 8

Photo 9

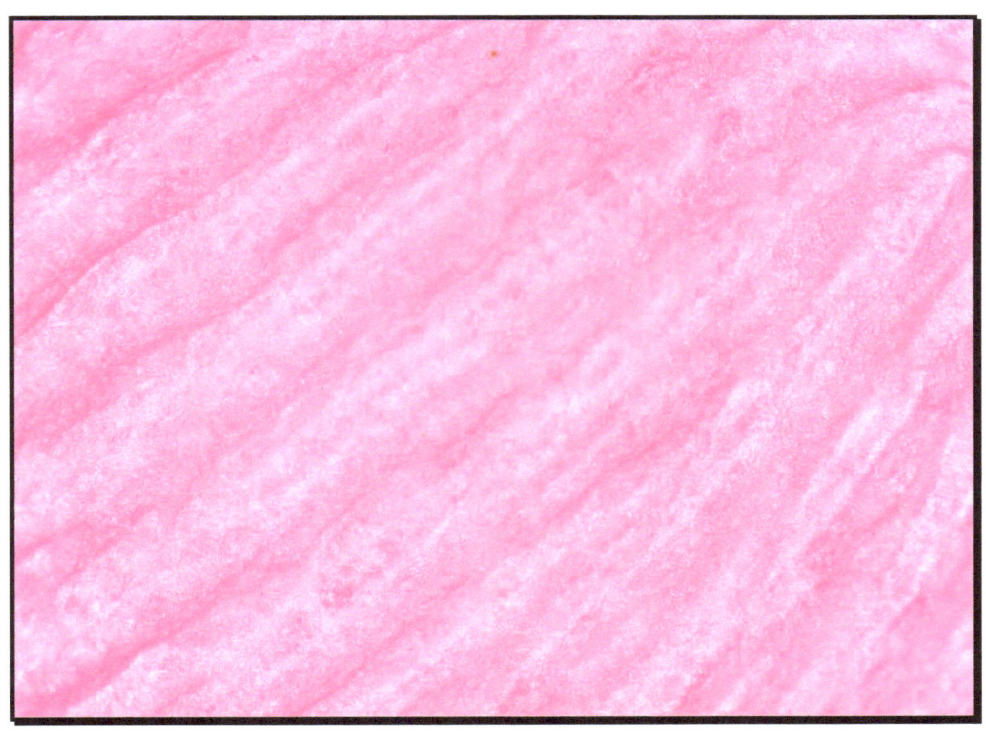

Photo 10

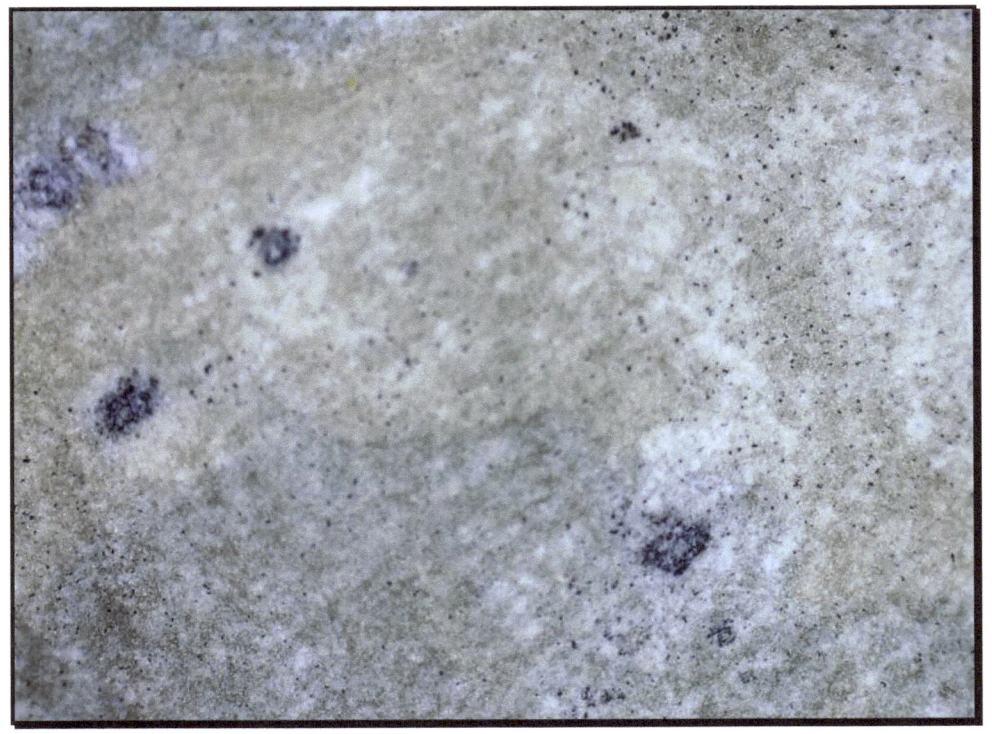

Photo 11

Photo 11 - Closer Look

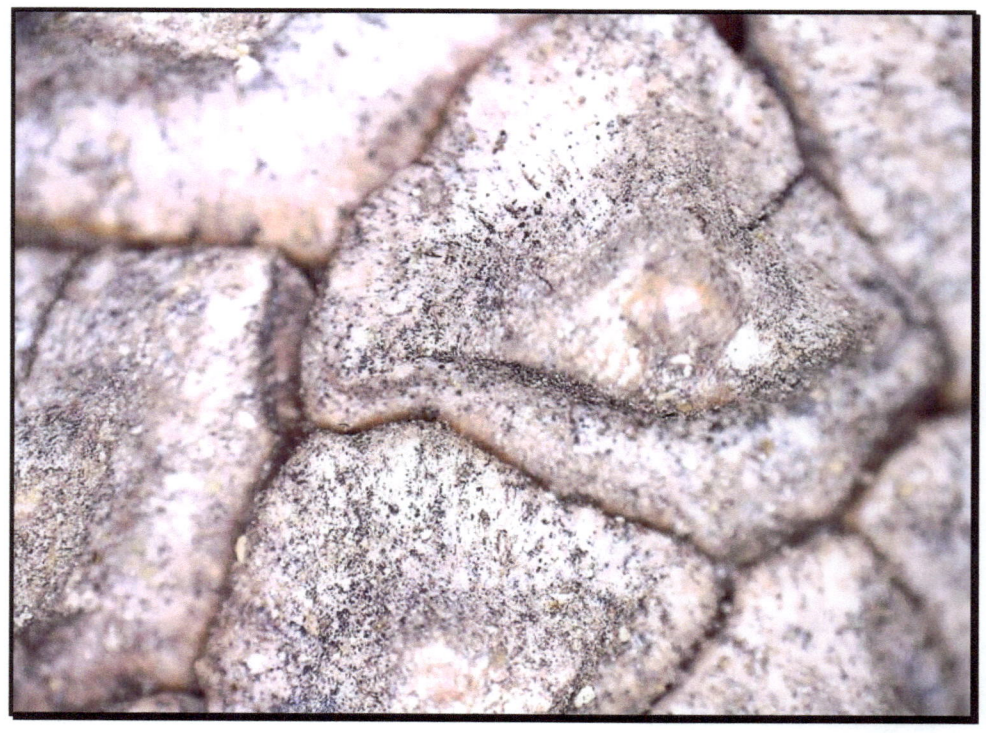

Photo 12

10

Photo 13

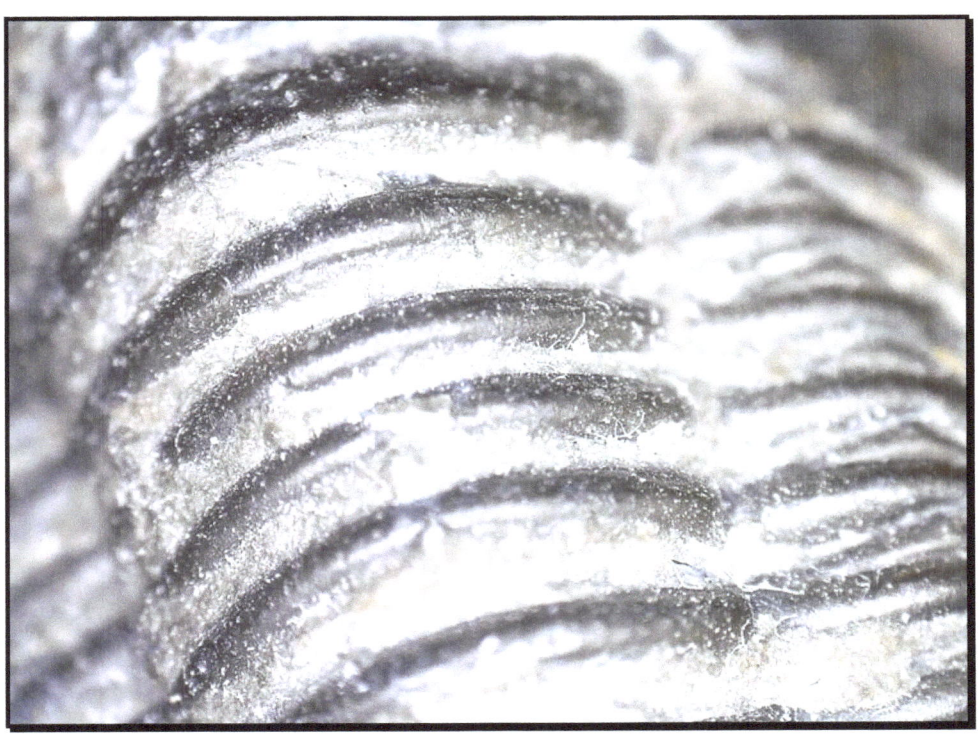

Photo 14

Photo 15

Photo 15 - A Closer Look

Photo 16

Photo 17

13

Photo 18

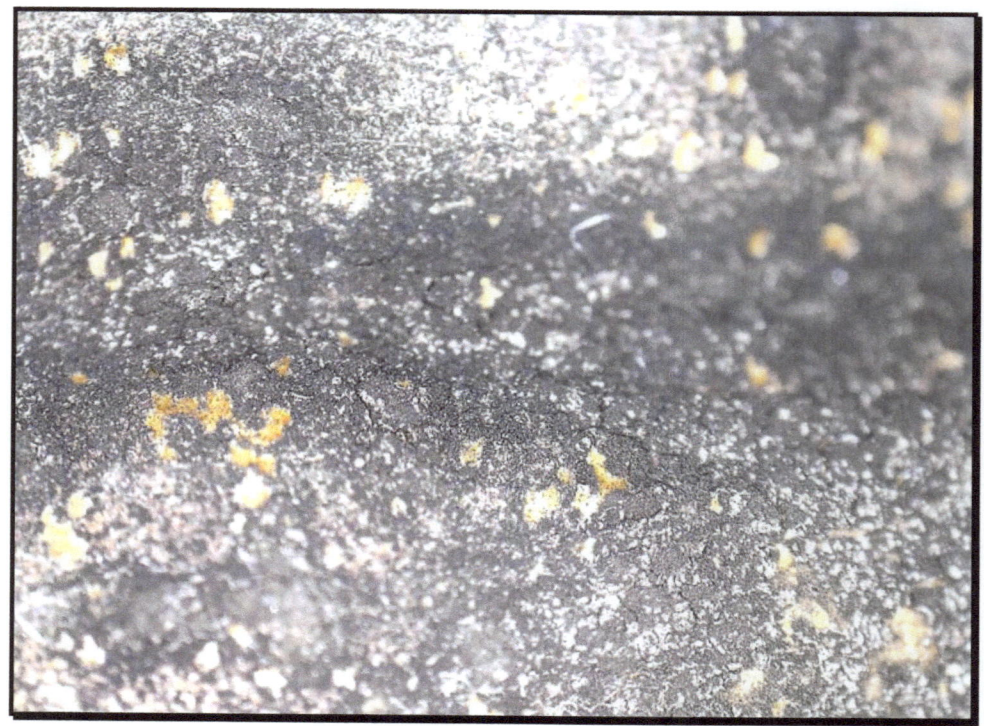

Photo 18 - A Closer Look

Photo 19

Photo 20

Photo 20 - A Closer Look

Photo 21

Photo 21 - A Closer Look

Photo 22

Photo 23

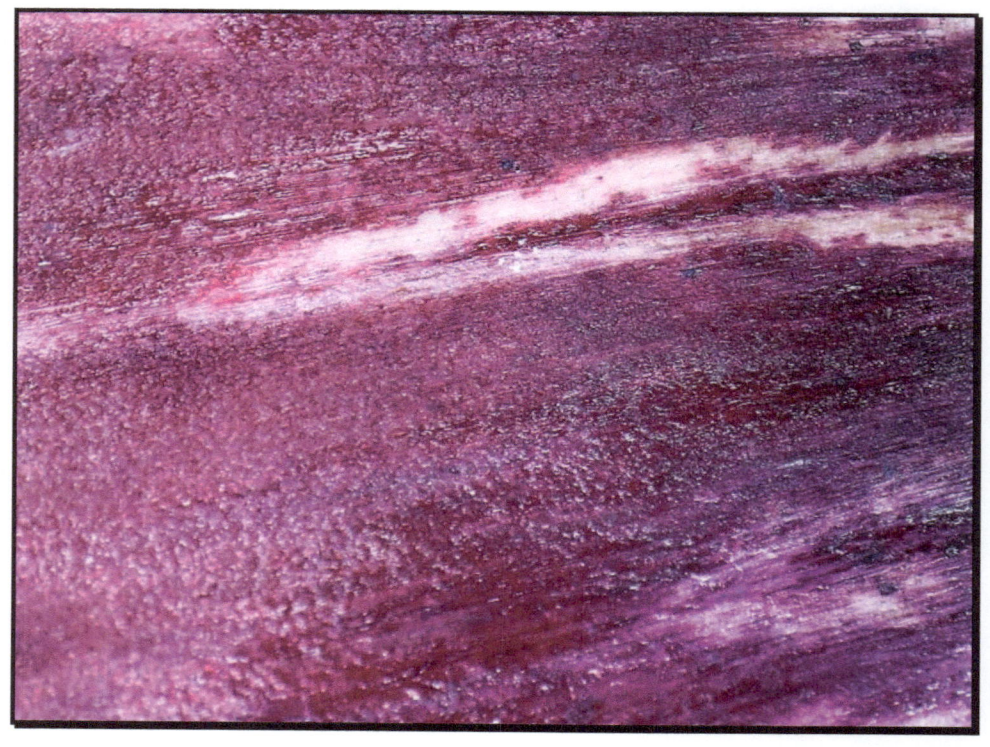

Photo 24

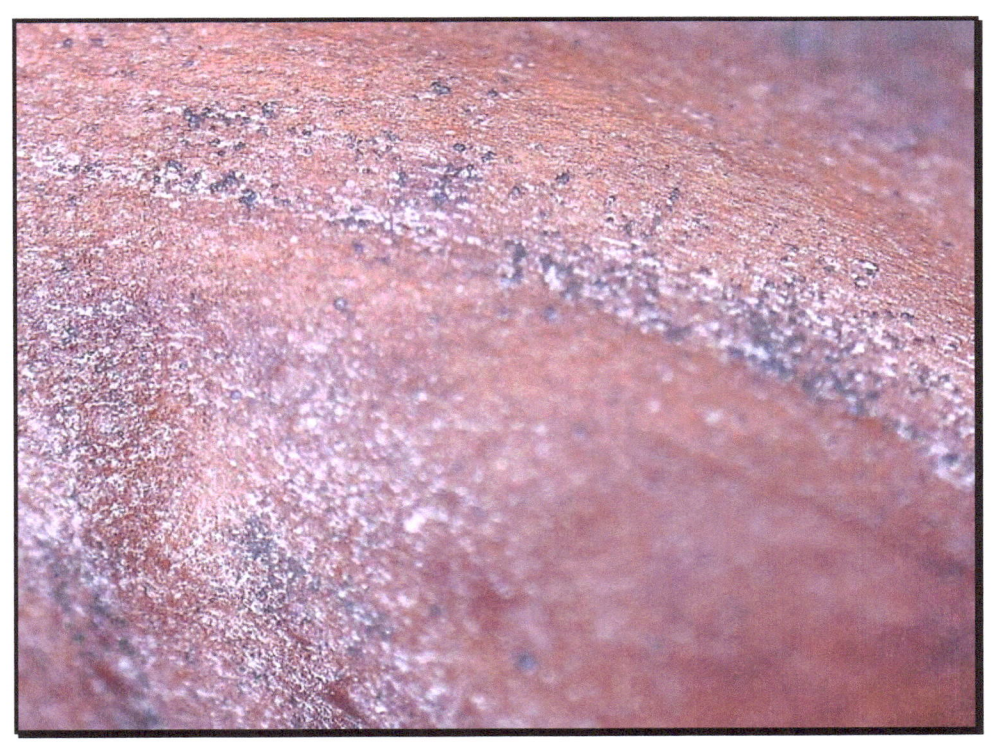

Photo 25

Photo 26

Photo 27

Photo 28

20

Photo 29

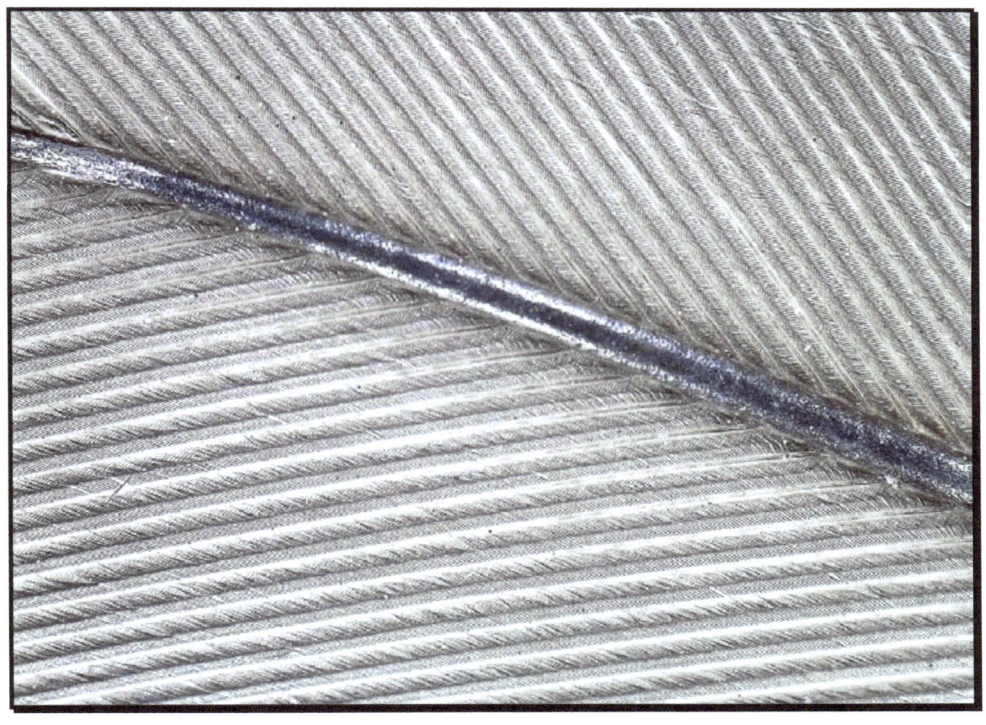

Photo 30

Photo 31

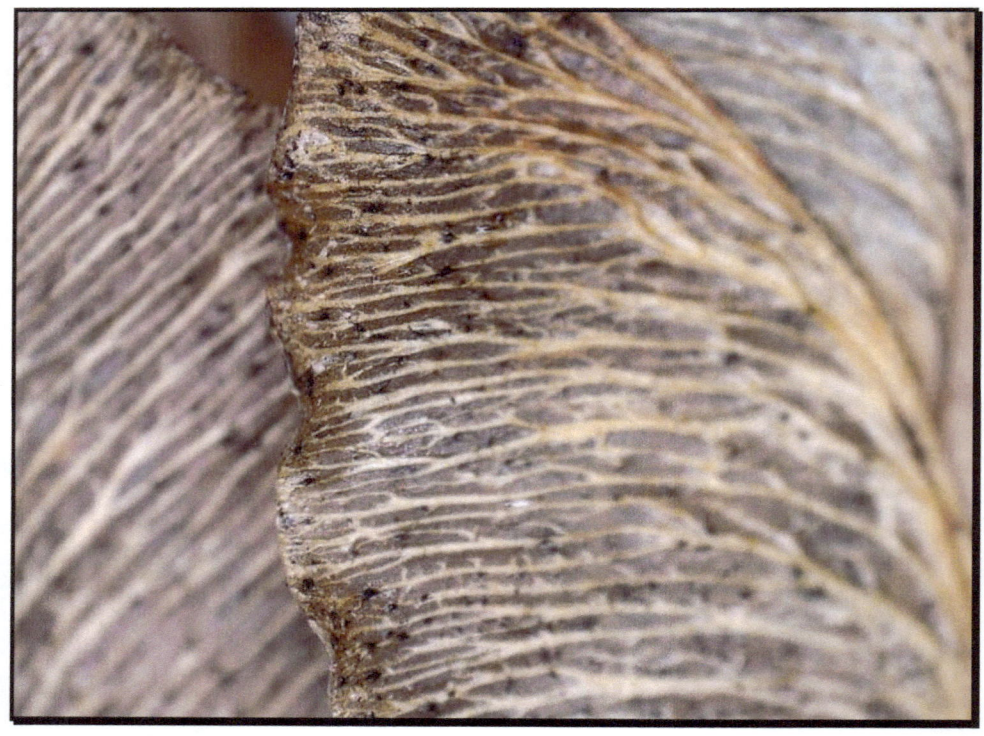

Photo 32

Photo 33

Photo 34

Photo 34 - A Closer Look

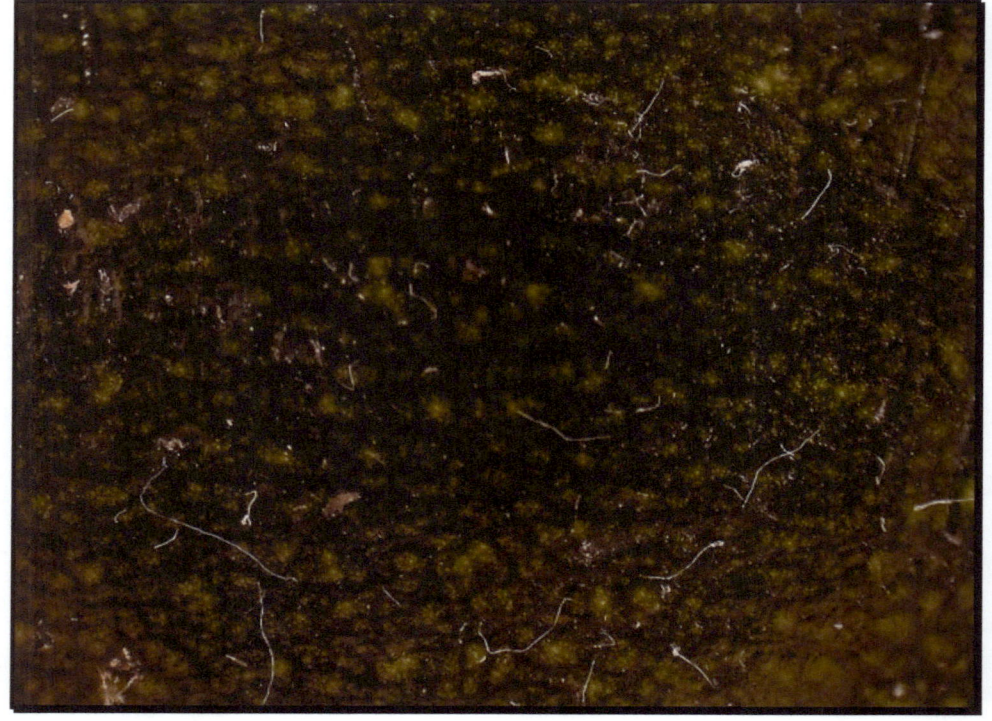

Photo 35

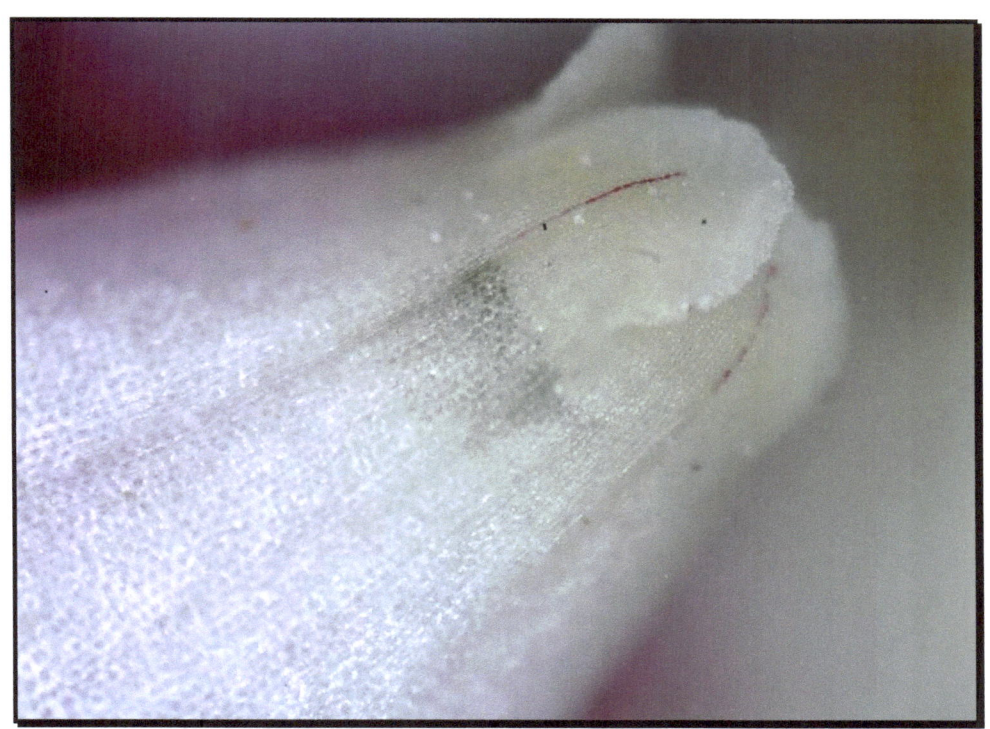

Photo 36

Photo 37

Photo 38

Photo 39 - Bottom

Photo 39 - Top

Photo 40

Photo 41

Photo 42

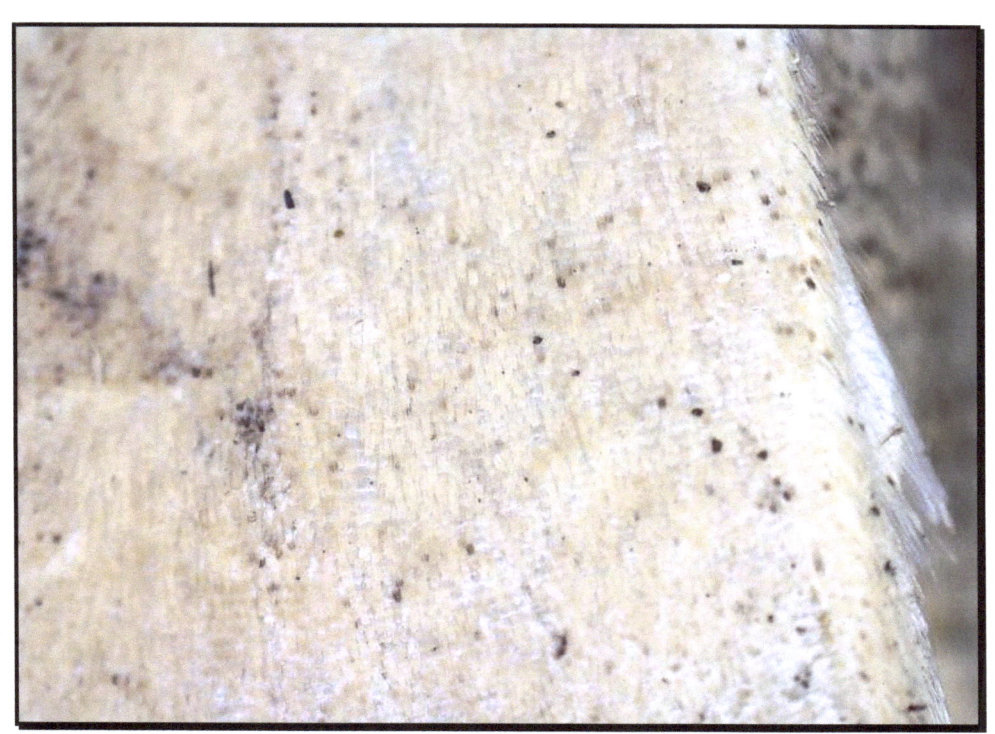

Photo 43

Photo 43

Photo 44

"Climb the mountains and get their good tidings. Nature's peace will flow into you as sunshine flows into trees. The winds will blow their own freshness into you, and the storms their energy, while cares will drop away from you like the leaves of autumn."
— John Muir, The Mountains of California

"Adopt the pace of nature: her secret is patience."
— Ralph Waldo Emerson

"Our task must be to free ourselves ... by widening our circle of compassion to embrace all living creatures and the whole of nature and it's beauty."
— Albert Einstein

"The best remedy for those who are afraid, lonely or unhappy is to go outside, somewhere where they can be quite alone with the heavens, nature and God. I firmly believe that nature brings solace in all troubles."
— Anne Frank, The Diary of a Young Girl

Photo 1. Seed Pod

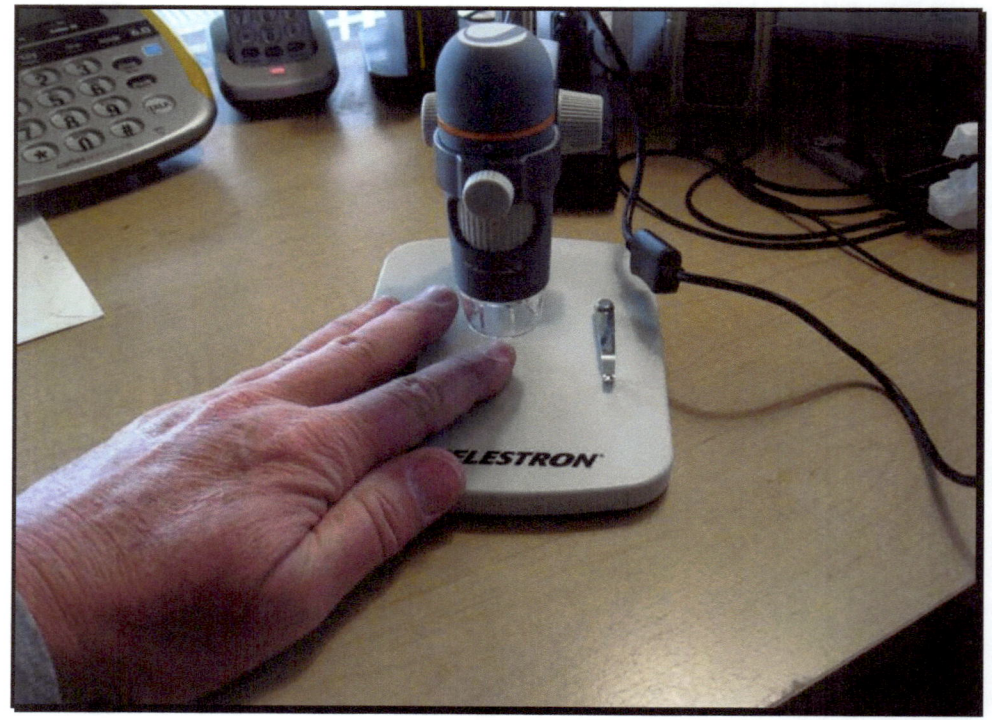

Photo 2. Fingernail

Photo 3. Dried up Prickly Pear Cactus

Photo 4. Manzanita Leaf

Photo 5. Ponderosa Pine Bark

Photo 6. Kiwi Fruit

Photo 7. Lichen

Photo 8. Herkimer Diamonds

Photo 9. Dried Century Plant Leaf

Photo 9. Dried Century Plant Leaf

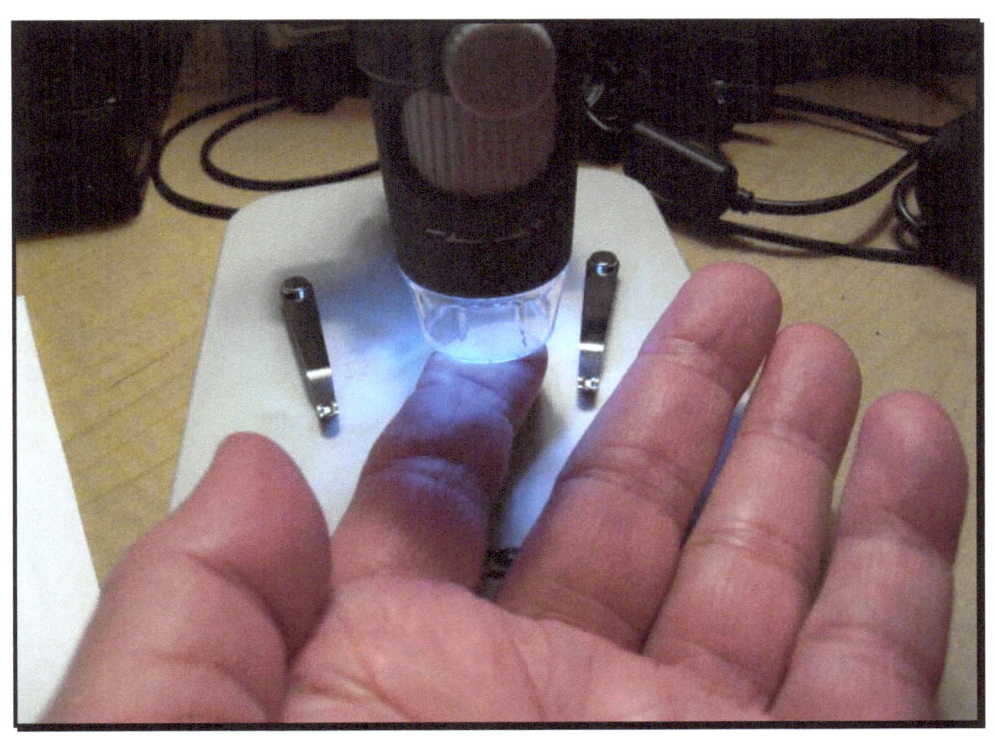

Photo 10. Fingerprint

Photo 11. Aspen Bark

Photo 12. Pinecone

Photo 13. Pine Sap

Photo 14. Trilobite

Photo 15. Mycelium

39

Photo 15. Mycelium

Photo 16. Lichen

Photo 17. Dried Aspen Bark

Photo 18. Century Plant Seed Pod

Photo 18. Century Plant Seed Pod

Photo 19. Pinecone with Spikes

Photo 20. Moss

Photo 21. Mullein

43

Photo 21. Mullein Leaf

Photo 22. Scrub Oak Bark

Photo 23. Feather with Contrasting Colors

Photo 24. Red Onion

Photo 25. Manzanita Bark

Photo 26. Volcanic Rock

Photo 27. Oak Leaf

Photo 28. Algae

Photo 28. Algae

Photo 29. Stinging Moss. Looks like soft velvety moss but if you touch it
you will get stung. I found out the hard way!

Photo 30. Beautiful White Feather

Photo 31. Juniper Berry

Photo 31. Juniper Berry

Photo 32. Seeds

Photo 33. Peanut

Photo 34. Prickly Pear Fruit

Photo 35. Zucchini Squash

Photo 36. Manzanita Flower

Photo 36. Manzanita Flower

Photo 37. Grass Seed

Photo 37. Grass Seed

Photo 38. Oak Burl

Photo 39. Fungus Top

Photo 39. Fungus Bottom

Photo 40. Bone

Photo 41. Acorn Cap

Photo 42. Seed Pods

Photo 42. Seed Pods

Photo 43. Moth

Photo. 43 Moth

Photo 44. Seed Sphere

Photo 44. Seed Sphere

Meet the Author

Hi, I'm Rick McKeon. I am currently living in beautiful Prescott, Arizona. Since retiring I have been spending time pursuing my passion for writing, playing music and teaching. I am currently producing a series of video lessons on playing the banjo and guitar, and am writing books encouraging people to appreciate nature at a deeper level.

Some of my other pursuits include hiking, backpacking, treasure hunting, exploring old ghost towns and mines, recreational mathematics, photography and experimenting with Microcontrollers.

For more about these activities check my other websites at rickmckeonNature.com and rickmckeonScientific.com

Other Books by this Author

Understanding Nature: Use All of Your Senses to Understand Nature at a Deeper Level!
ISBN: 9781311565129

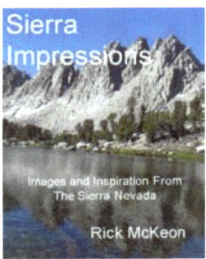

Sierra Impressions: Images and Inspiration From the Sierras
ISBN: 9781310403699

Underlying Patterns: The Search for Patterns in Nature
ISBN: 9781311783615

You Make Us Feel Young Again!
ISBN: 9781310558108

Amazing Fractal Images: Postcards From the Complex Plane
ISBN: 9781311990440